20TH CENTURY AMERICAN WOMEN'S HISTORY FOR KIDS

20th CENTURY

AMERICAN WOMEN'S HISTORY

FOR Kids

the MAJOR EVENTS THAT SHAPED the PAST and PRESENT

CARRIE FLOYD CAGLE

ROCKRIDGE
PRESS

Series Designer: Michael Patti
Interior and Cover Designer: Regina Stadnik
Art Producer: Hannah Dickerson
Editor: Barbara J. Isenberg
Production Editor: Mia Moran
Production Manager: Holly Haydash

Illustration © 2021 Jonathan Ball, cover and p. III; All other illustrations used under license from Shutterstock.com. Photography © Niday Picture Library/Alamy Stock Photo, back cover and p. 44; Everett Collection Inc/Alamy Stock Photo, pp. 4, 24; IanDagnall Computing/Alamy Stock Photo, p. 5; UPI/Alamy Stock Photo, pp. 7, 84; Harris & Ewing photograph collection, Prints & Photographs Division, Library of Congress, LC-DIG-hec-10555, p. 10; Underwood & Underwood, Prints & Photographs Division, Library of Congress, LC-USZ62-58972, p. 13; Historic Collection/Alamy Stock Photo, p. 14; Harris & Ewing photograph collection, Prints & Photographs Division, Library of Congress, LC-DIG-hec-18526, p. 16; Manuscript Division, Library of Congress, http://hdl.loc.gov/loc.mss/mnwp.276016, p. 19; Photo 12/Alamy Stock Photo, p. 25; Harris & Ewing photograph collection, Prints & Photographs Division, Library of Congress, LC-DIG-hec-44086, p. 27; Dorothea Lange, Farm Security Administration - Office of War Information Photograph Collection, Prints & Photographs Division, Library of Congress, LC-USF34-T01-009093-C, p. 30; Everett Collection Historical/Alamy Stock Photo, pp. 33, 50, 70; Harris & Ewing photograph collection, Prints & Photographs Division, Library of Congress, LC-DIG-hec-23686, p. 36; Harris & Ewing photograph collection, Prints & Photographs Division, Library of Congress, LC-DIG-hec-25100, p. 37; Alpha Historica/Alamy Stock Photo, p. 39; The Picture Art Collection/Alamy Stock Photo, p. 47; New York World-Telegram and the Sun Newspaper Photograph Collection, Prints & Photographs Division, Library of Congress, LC-USZC2-5838, p. 53; PictureLux/The Hollywood Archive/Alamy Stock Photo, p. 56; AF archive/Alamy Stock Photo, p. 57; Pictorial Press Ltd/Alamy Stock Photo, p. 59; Universal Art Archive/Alamy Stock Photo, p. 64; Science History Images/Alamy Stock Photo, pp. 65, 73, 77; Glasshouse Images/Alamy Stock Photo, p. 67; Keystone Press/Alamy Stock Photo, p. 76; Bettmann/Getty Images, p. 79; NASA Photo/Alamy Stock Photo, p. 87; Sueddeutsche Zeitung Photo/Alamy Stock Photo, p. 90; RBM Vintage Images/Alamy Stock Photo, p. 93; Richard Ellis/Alamy Stock Photo, p. 96; REUTERS/Alamy Stock Photo, p. 99; ZUMA Press, Inc./Alamy Stock Photo, p. 100.

Paperback ISBN: 978-1-64876-759-3 | eBook ISBN: 978-1-64876-760-9
R0

"YOU DON'T MAKE PROGRESS
BY STANDING ON THE SIDELINES,
WHIMPERING AND COMPLAINING.
YOU MAKE PROGRESS
BY IMPLEMENTING IDEAS."

—*Shirley Chisholm*

CONTENTS

INTRODUCTION

I remember a bulletin board that hung in my elementary school hallway during Women's History Month. It sported a cheesy title: "History? Herstory? OUR STORY." Underneath the title were pictures of three different women: Betsy Ross, Amelia Earhart, and Nancy Reagan, the First Lady of the United States at the time.

Though it may seem unremarkable, this bulletin board tells us a lot about the purpose of studying women's history. First, the title: "history" *does* start with "his." Until about 30 years ago, most history books were only about the achievements of important—usually white—men. History was seen as a series of events related to male politicians, military generals, inventors, and scientists. Very little was written about what women had accomplished. This was partly because women were often not allowed to be educated or participate in politics, so they had to work extra hard to achieve the same things that men could.

This doesn't mean that what women did was not important. Women make up slightly more than half of the population. A historical education that is only about half of the people isn't complete! Forgive the silly pun, but we do need to add a "herstory" to tell "our story."

Second, why learn about women's history only during March? Women exist year-round! History should represent them year-round, too. We all want to learn about role models who resemble ourselves. That means history should also include Black people, **Latinx**, **Indigenous** people, people who are disabled, Asian people, **LGBTQ** people, and so on.

Finally, only *three* women were included on that bulletin board! This book includes just some of the most important events in American women's history in the 20th century. You can learn more about women's history by checking the Resources at the back of this book. My hope is that once you've read this book, you will be able to fill 10 bulletin boards with accomplished American women from diverse backgrounds.

WOMEN IN THE UNITED STATES AT THE TURN OF THE 20th CENTURY

I n the 1800s and early 1900s, a lot of people believed that women were morally superior to men. Business, politics, and higher education were all considered too difficult for women.

Before the 20th century, which started in 1901, most homes didn't include *any* modern household appliances. Women did every task by hand. They cooked meals from scratch, hand-washed dishes, baked bread, wove cloth, sewed clothes, swept floors, did laundry, cleaned windows, tended crops—and more!

Before the Civil War, some women got involved with the antislavery movement, which argued that Black men should have equality with white men. This led Elizabeth Cady Stanton and Lucretia Mott to question women's lack of equality, too.

In 1848, Stanton and Mott organized the Seneca Falls Convention. This is considered the first American women's rights convention. Those who attended agreed that women should be allowed to own property, have educations equal to those of men, and, most important, gain suffrage, or the right to vote. These goals inspired **activists** to form several other women's suffrage organizations.

CHAPTER ONE

1901
TO
1920

The first two decades of the 20th century included two big themes: **industrialization** and **progressivism**.

Industrialization happens when a society that makes goods by hand starts making them in factories. This is usually paired with

urbanization, the movement of people from rural areas to cities.

These changes began in the United States in the 1800s. By the 1900s, they were beginning to have important effects on the country. One positive effect was **economic** growth. The United States was becoming wealthier and trading with many countries. But not everyone shared in this new wealth. Many of the factory workers who made industrialization possible lived and worked in horrible conditions.

The second theme, progressivism, was based on the idea that people and government should work together to solve problems in society. Reformers organized groups that focused on specific problems. They were called "reformers" because they wanted to re-form, or re-shape, the way their communities worked.

Reformers concentrated on making workplaces safer, keeping food and medicine pure, and making the government more democratic. This included expanding the right to vote, so the women's rights organizations fit right in!

A committee of the National League of Women Voters in 1924

New Leaders in the Suffrage Movement: 1900

Along with the new century came new leaders in the suffrage movement. Suffrage means the right to vote in elections. Women had been fighting for the right to vote since the 1840s, but by 1900, they still hadn't succeeded. Susan B. Anthony was an early leader in the movement and president of the National American Woman Suffrage Association (NAWSA). However, she retired as the president in 1900 and died soon after in 1906. Several other early women's rights leaders—like Elizabeth Cady Stanton, Lucy Stone, and Lucretia Mott—had already passed away.

In 1900, Carrie Chapman Catt took over leadership of NAWSA. She and Anna Howard Shaw led the organization for the next 20 years. NAWSA's plan was to get women the right to vote in state elections. Eventually, they would work on getting them the right to vote in national elections.

Two younger activists, Alice Paul and Lucy Burns, also joined NAWSA. Paul and Burns had gone to college in England. There, they had worked with English suffrage workers and learned **militant** tactics. The English women picketed and went on hunger strikes. Picketing involves a group of people chanting, marching, and holding up signs outside a public place. In a hunger strike, protestors refuse to eat in order to make others feel guilty about the policy they are protesting.

MEET MARY CHURCH TERRELL

Mary Church Terrell was the daughter of formerly enslaved people who worked for equal rights and suffrage for Black people. Though NAWSA didn't officially forbid Black women to join, many state and local units of the organization refused to admit them. Terrell helped found two organizations that worked toward ending discrimination against Black people—the National Association of Colored Women in 1896 and the National Association for the Advancement of Colored People in 1909.

These more active and aggressive tactics were not NAWSA's style. Also, Paul and Burns wanted to concentrate on getting the national vote right away. They formed their own organization, the National Women's Party (NWP).

Another activist, Harriot Stanton Blatch, noticed that mostly upper- and middle-class women were involved in the suffrage movement. She wanted to involve **working-class** women as well, so she founded the Equality League of Self-Supporting Women. Later, this group merged with the NWP.

These new leaders of the suffrage movement had a big impact. They got more women involved and protested their lack of rights more actively. By 1920, they would achieve their goal.

WOMEN AGAINST WOMEN'S SUFFRAGE?

Though it may be difficult for us to believe, there *were* women who were against suffrage in the early 20th century. Some said women were too busy in the home and did not have extra time to keep up with politics. Other common arguments were that women's brains were too delicate to understand politics and that they might vote differently than their husbands did and hurt their marriages.

The Triangle Shirtwaist Factory fire

Triangle Shirtwaist Factory Fire: 1911

While some women worked hard to win the vote, other women worked hard simply to earn a living. In big cities like New York City and Chicago, factories employed thousands of **immigrants**, people who had just moved to the United States from other countries.

Life was very hard for immigrants from certain parts of Europe, like Italy, Russia, and Greece. Americans were **prejudiced** against them. Immigrants often had to take low-paying jobs in unsafe conditions.

The Triangle Shirtwaist Factory in New York City was one place where immigrant women worked

MEET ROSE SCHNEIDERMAN

Rose Schneiderman was a Polish immigrant. Because of her family's **poverty**, her mother was forced to send her to a New York City orphanage. She started out working a machine in a hat factory. Eventually, she became the first woman president of the New York Women's Trade Union League (NYWTUL). Schneiderman gave a moving speech after the fire at the Triangle Shirtwaist Factory. Her speech motivated the NYWTUL and others to continue working to improve conditions for factory workers.

extremely long hours for very low pay. The workers made ladies' blouses under terrible, unsafe conditions. Employees were locked inside the factory every day while they worked to keep them from taking too many breaks. The factory was located on the 8th, 9th, and 10th floors of a 10-story building.

On March 25, 1911, a fire started on the 8th floor. Some of the women on the 8th and 10th floors of the factory were able to escape using the stairs and elevators. But there was no way to contact the workers on the 9th floor, where the doors were locked.

Some of the workers tried to use the fire escape, which was already broken. It collapsed. Sixty-two young women jumped from the windows and fell to their deaths on the sidewalks. The rest remained on the 9th floor and died in the fire. A total of 146 people were killed that day.

As a result of the tragedy, the state of New York began to check factories and pass laws to make them safer for all workers. Also, more women joined the International Ladies' Garment Workers' Union (ILGWU). A **union** is a group of workers who agree to work together to bargain with their bosses for better working conditions. The ILGWU was one of the first and largest American labor unions to have mostly female members.

THE UPRISING OF THE 20,000

About a year and a half before the fire at the Triangle Shirtwaist Factory, 20,000 workers who were part of the ILGWU went on **strike**. They were protesting their long workweek, low pay, and unsafe working conditions. In February 1910, factory owners gave in to their demands. The owners must not have made enough changes, though, or the Triangle fire would not have been so deadly.

Girl Scouts sewing in 1915

Girl Scouts of America: 1912

Juliette Gordon Low grew up in Savannah, Georgia. As a child, she loved being outdoors, learning about animals and nature. On a visit to England in 1912, she met Robert Baden-Powell, the founder of the Boy Scouts.

Low wanted to start a similar group for girls in America, so she formed the first American Girl Scout troop in Savannah in 1912. Her goal was to prepare girls for anything they might need to know as women. Low knew most of the girls would be wives and mothers, so she taught them about cooking, sewing, and nursing sick children. She also knew life could be unpredictable. Many women might have to be able to support themselves at some point, so she also emphasized career training.

Low wanted girls to get fresh air and enjoy physical activity. Girl Scouts played basketball and tennis on her land in Savannah. This was not usual for girls at the time. Low hung up a curtain so that people walking by would not see the girls and be offended. This only made people more curious about the organization!

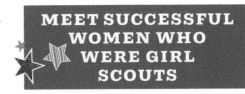

MEET SUCCESSFUL WOMEN WHO WERE GIRL SCOUTS

Many well-known women were Girl Scouts! TV host Martha Stewart; actor and musician Queen Latifah; tennis player Venus Williams; former First Lady Michelle Obama; former First Lady, senator, and presidential candidate Hillary Clinton; actors Dakota Fanning, Vanessa Hudgens, Gwyneth Paltrow, and Carrie Fisher; and musician Taylor Swift are just a few of the women who once wore the green vest.

Another thing the Girl Scouts did that was unusual for the time was to mix girls of different backgrounds. Upper-class, middle-class, and working-class girls; immigrant girls, Black girls, and white girls—all types of girls joined the Scouts. By 1913, the Girl Scouts of

America had expanded to many other states. By the 1920s, there were troops on almost every continent.

Low died in 1927, but the Girl Scouts continued to grow. Today, it is the world's largest organization devoted to girls' leadership. Researchers have even done studies on how being a Girl Scout affects girls' lives. They have found that girls who were Girl Scouts are more likely to participate in their communities and volunteer. They also are more successful in their educations and careers. Clearly, the Girl Scouts has made a big impact on a lot of girls' lives!

THE HISTORY OF GIRL SCOUT COOKIES

The first Girl Scout cookies were home-baked by a troop in Muskogee, Oklahoma, in 1917. The troop sold the cookies in their high school cafeteria. Five years later, a Girl Scouts magazine featured an inexpensive cookie recipe that allowed troops around the country to bake and sell their own cookies. In 1935, the first bakery-made cookies were sold, and people are still eating Girl Scout cookies to this day!

Suffragists in Washington, DC in 1913

Women's Suffrage Parade in Washington, DC: 1913

Whereas American girls were learning to be independent in the Girl Scouts, American women were marching in protest of their lack of voting rights. By 1913, women suffragists Alice Paul and Lucy Burns were growing impatient. Their organization's strategy was to win the vote for women state by state, using written arguments and speeches. But Paul and Burns hoped to use more dramatic methods to gain national suffrage. They began planning a huge parade to be held in Washington, DC.

The parade was planned for a very important date: March 3. This was the day before President Woodrow Wilson's **inauguration**. Paul knew that there would

MEET MARIE LOUISE BOTTINEAU BALDWIN

Marie Louise Bottineau Baldwin, a member of the Turtle Mountain Band of the Chippewa Nation, worked as a clerk for the Office of Indian Affairs. She wore her traditional native clothing at work and when she marched in the 1913 parade. This symbolized her support for her Indigenous culture. It also attracted reporters, who interviewed her about suffrage for Indigenous women. Indigenous peoples were not made citizens until 1924 and could not vote in all states until 1962. Baldwin eventually became a lawyer and went on to become a leading member of the Society of American Indians.

be many people in town that day. She also knew that the parade would take attention away from President Wilson.

The route for the parade was carefully planned so it would receive maximum attention. The marchers would proceed straight down Pennsylvania Avenue, marching right in front of the White House.

The organizers of the parade designed it to be visually stunning. It was led by Inez Milholland, a lawyer, who rode a white horse. More than 20 floats and groups of women followed her. The groups of women represented different achievements of modern women. Before the parade, women had seemed to be politely asking for the vote. But now, they demanded it.

Very soon after the parade began, people from the sidewalks began to move into the street. They blocked the parade route and harassed the marchers. Police officers nearby either would not or could not help. The women marched as well as they could anyway until the US Army showed up to clear the parade route.

The parade did exactly what Paul and Burns had planned—it stole publicity from Woodrow Wilson's inauguration. It also led Congress to reintroduce debate about women's suffrage for the first time in decades.

BLACK WOMEN IN THE PROCESSION

The organizers of the parade were torn about whether to allow Black women to march because Washington, DC, was **segregated**. Finally, they decided to include Black women in a segregated group in the back. Many people called and wrote to protest this separation of Black and white women. As a result of the calls, around 50 Black women marched side-by-side with their white allies in their state organizations.

Congresswoman Jeannette Rankin

First Woman Elected to Congress: 1916

Before Jeannette Rankin became involved with the women's suffrage movement, she worked in several states in many different jobs. Later, she became a national field secretary for the National American Woman Suffrage Association.

Rankin was very good at organizing. In almost every state where she worked on a campaign, women won the vote. After women gained suffrage in her home state of Montana, she decided to run for Congress there in 1916.

World War I had already started by then, though the United States was not yet officially involved. Rankin thought it was important that America stay out of the war. She also wanted to gain national support for suffrage and better working conditions for all kinds of laborers. She had to travel a lot to talk to potential voters because

MEET HATTIE CARAWAY

Hattie Caraway first became a senator in 1931 when her husband, Democrat Thaddeus Caraway, died in office. The Arkansas governor appointed her to fill her husband's seat. In 1932 and 1938, she ran for election in her own right and won. This made her the first woman to be elected to the Senate. She also became the first woman to chair a Senate committee and the first woman to run a Senate hearing.

Montana was a large state with a small population. Montana had two seats in the House of Representatives, and Rankin came in second place in the election. This meant she was elected to Congress for the second seat! She was now the *only* woman in the nation with **federal** voting power.

On her first day in Congress, Rankin introduced her first bill: to amend the Constitution to give women suffrage across the nation. By this time, 40 out of the

48 states allowed women to vote in state elections. Soon after, President Wilson proposed declaring war on Germany. This took attention away from all other matters. Rankin voted against getting involved in the war.

Later in her term, Rankin became one of the founding members of the House Committee on Woman Suffrage. Unfortunately, her term ended before women gained nationwide suffrage. Since her election, as of 2021, a total of 393 women have served in Congress.

THE WIDOW'S MANDATE

Historically, when a congressman died in office, his wife could take over his seat through a special election or the governor's appointment until his term was up. This practice was called the "widow's mandate." To date, 47 women have entered Congress this way. Some of these women were able to run for and win reelection. This custom served as an important entryway to Congress for women.

Suffragists demonstrating in 1916

19th Amendment Is Ratified: 1920

The **Constitution of the United States** is the written document that describes how the United States government works. It was written in 1787, when life was very different than it is now. The men who wrote it knew that it might need to be changed to keep up with modern times. The way to change the Constitution is to add an amendment. In order for this to happen, two-thirds of each house of Congress must vote to propose the amendment. Then three-quarters of the states must vote to ratify, or approve, the amendment.

Up until 1919, women had been slowly gaining the right to vote in state elections. That meant they could vote in elections for their state governors or in local elections for mayors or city councils.

In order for women to be able to vote in national elections for Congress or president, an amendment had to be added to the Constitution. A California senator, Aaron Sargent, first suggested such an amendment to Congress in 1878. Unfortunately, there wasn't enough interest at the time. Congress considered women's suffrage several other times between then and 1919, but there wasn't enough support for it.

Then, in 1918, President Woodrow Wilson began to publicly support suffrage. Women had made great contributions during World War I. President Wilson felt that he couldn't deny them the vote after that. With his support, the 19th Amendment was proposed in 1919, and the states ratified it in 1920. Finally, women had the vote!

Well . . . *some* women had the vote. Some groups, including Black people in the South and Indigenous people, were still not able to vote. This meant that mostly white women benefited from the passage of the 19th Amendment.

THE FINAL VOTE

By August 18, 1920, the Senate had already ratified the 19th Amendment. In the House of Representatives, though, the amendment needed just one vote from Tennessee to be ratified. The atmosphere was tense when a messenger showed up with a note for Harry Burn. Burn, a senator from Tennessee, was anti-suffrage. But the message from his mother, Phoebe King Ensminger Burn, changed his mind— she asked him to vote for suffrage. He then cast the winning vote for women's suffrage.

CHAPTER TWO

1921 TO 1940

From 1914 to 1918, the most powerful countries in the world were at war in World War I. The warring countries needed supplies, like guns, bullets, and tanks. American factories were able to make the supplies and sell them to the warring countries. Factory workers were paid well. The factory owners also made money from selling their goods. As a result, many Americans enjoyed a period of **prosperity** that lasted throughout most of the 1920s.

Not everyone who had extra money was responsible with it. Some people bought items on **credit** that they couldn't really afford. Investors put too much confidence in the stock market. Meanwhile, farmers began to have trouble selling their crops.

The 1920s were a time when many new inventions and ideas became popular. Yet some people were concerned that there were too many changes happening at once. This led to cultural conflict—Americans could not agree on how people should behave and think.

In 1929, the stock market crashed. This caused unemployment, homelessness, and hunger. This time period, called the Great Depression, continued throughout the 1930s.

Franklin D. Roosevelt was elected president in 1932. He convinced Congress to pass a series of laws called the New Deal to help those in need. The New Deal made the Depression a little better, but there were still problems until 1939.

A Flapper and her date on the cover of *Life* magazine in 1926

The Rise of the Flapper: 1920s

Until the 1920s, American women were expected to dress and act a certain way. Everything had to be long—long dresses, long sleeves, long hair. Beneath their dresses, women wore corsets—supportive undergarments with whalebones sewn in. A corset could squeeze the wearer's waist to a very small size. The compression of the corsets and the heavy clothing could make women hot and uncomfortable. Unmarried women had to be very careful about how they acted in public with men. If a single woman wanted to spend time with a man, she had to have a chaperone. As you can imagine, this made courtship—the process of getting to know a romantic partner—a bit awkward!

Along came flappers! Flappers were young women who rebelled against the restrictions. They threw away their corsets, wore knee-length skirts, cut their hair short, and wore a lot of makeup. They smoked cigarettes and drank alcohol in public. Jazz was a very popular style of music at the time, and flappers danced suggestively in jazz clubs. Chaperones were not a concern for flappers, either. Not all women could be flappers, though. It was a very expensive lifestyle!

MEET JOSEPHINE BAKER

Josephine Baker was a flapper, entertainer, and **civil rights** activist. As a jazz singer and dancer, she refused to perform in clubs that segregated audience members. She was the first Black American woman to star in a major film. Baker moved to France in 1925 to escape the racism in the United States. Still, she frequently spoke out for equality for Black people in the United States. Baker was the only official female speaker at the March on Washington, an important civil rights event in 1963.

Clara Bow was the most well-known flapper. She was an actor who starred in 57 films. She became famous from a movie called *It*, so she was often called "the It Girl." Other famous flappers included Zelda Fitzgerald and Josephine Baker.

The flappers' behavior doesn't seem very shocking today. But in the 1920s, "the new woman" seemed horrifying and immoral to some. Over time, most people got used to these new ways of dressing and behaving, and women were able to have more freedoms. Modern women can thank flappers for helping make it acceptable to be more independent and to wear more comfortable clothing.

LAS PELONAS: LATINA FLAPPERS

The flapper style appealed to young women of various backgrounds. Spanish-speaking Americans called flappers *las pelonas*, which means "short-haired girls." Like all flappers, las pelonas were viewed as going against the traditional values of their communities. Spanish-language newspapers also criticized them for being "too American" and forgetting their own heritage.

Politician Myrtle Cain supporting the Equal Rights Amendment in 1924

Equal Rights Amendment: 1923

As you read in chapter 1 (page 19), the 19th Amendment gave women the right to vote in 1921. Soon after, Alice Paul, the leader of the National Woman's Party (NWP), had a question for its members. She asked if they thought their work was finished, and they answered "no!"

Women still faced discrimination. They could not work in certain jobs or be paid as much as men were. They could be fired from a job for becoming pregnant. Some states did not allow women to own property. Many states kept Black women from voting. Nothing in the Constitution made discrimination against women illegal. So, the NWP chose to support the passing of a new amendment called the Equal Rights Amendment (ERA).

The ERA was worded very simply: "Men and women shall have equal rights throughout the United States." This meant that the national and state governments would have to make sure that women were treated in the same way men were treated. If there were a situation in which women were discriminated against, the government would have to put a stop to it.

Surprisingly, some women's rights activists were *against* the proposed amendment. They were especially concerned about laws that protected female workers. These laws did things like limit the number of hours women and children could work. If women and men were to be treated equally, then these laws could no longer be enforced. Opponents worried that without these safeguards, women would face more dangerous working conditions.

Despite these arguments, the NWP was determined to have the amendment introduced to Congress. It just so happened that Susan B. Anthony's nephew, Daniel Anthony Jr., was a representative for Kansas. He presented the amendment on December 13, 1923. Most of the members of Congress at that time were men. They were not ready to give equal rights to women, so the amendment did not pass. Women's rights activists did not forget about it, though. It would gain national attention again in the 1970s.

THE NATIONAL CONSUMERS LEAGUE

The National Consumers League's (NCL) goal was to promote the interests of both consumers—people who buy products—and workers. It supported limiting the working hours of women and children, which meant different rules for women and men. As a result, the NCL produced arguments against the Equal Rights Amendment in favor of protecting female workers.

A migrant woman and her two children photographed by Dorothea Lange in 1936

The Great Depression Begins: 1929

The Great Depression was a 10-year period when most people suffered from extreme money problems. It began in October 1929, when the stock market crashed. A stock is a small piece of a company that an individual can own. A stock market crash occurs when the value of all stocks goes down quickly.

When the stock market crashed, there was a decline in the value of money. This was a sign that some companies were running out of money. People lost their jobs. These unemployed people did not have the money to buy products or pay for housing. Because the banks weren't receiving housing payments, they ran out of money. Then more companies failed because people couldn't afford to buy their products. This created a cycle that kept making the Depression worse. Because other countries' economies were tied to the US economy, the Depression soon became a worldwide problem.

Many men who had been their families' main source of income could not find jobs. Ashamed, some simply abandoned their families. More women needed to work outside the home. Employers could pay women less than they paid men because there were no laws requiring equal pay. As a result, it was cheaper for companies to hire women.

Because new groups of women were competing for jobs, it was harder for poor women to find work. Many of these poor women were **people of color**—Black,

MEET DOROTHEA LANGE

Dorothea Lange was a trained photographer who took documentary photographs. These pictures show what life was really like, so they are not always pretty and happy. Her photos were so good that the government hired her to photograph the effects of the Great Depression on people around the United States. Lange is well known for her pictures of women and children in camps where farm workers and their families lived.

Latina, Asian American, and Indigenous people. They were often forced to take the lowest-paying jobs due to discrimination.

Meanwhile, women were still expected to take care of their household and children. Some children were left to fend for themselves while their mothers worked. Mothers were also the ones who had to figure out how to keep everyone fed and clothed on limited incomes.

Beginning in 1933, President Franklin D. Roosevelt and Congress passed a set of laws. These laws, called the New Deal, would allow the government to assist some of the people in need. The New Deal helped a little, but the Depression would not officially end in the United States until 1939 when World War II began.

MEXICAN AMERICANS IN THE GREAT DEPRESSION

Many Mexican Americans and Mexican immigrants worked as farm laborers in the 1920s. In 1929, when the Great Depression began, their fates changed. Some Americans thought that it was wrong for these immigrants to work when Americans were unemployed. As a result, the government began to "repatriate" the workers, forcing them to move back to Mexico.

Amelia Earhart turning the propeller of her sports plane

Founding of the Ninety-Nines: 1929

Americans officially took flight when Orville and Wilbur Wright flew their plane 120 feet in the air in Kitty Hawk, North Carolina, in 1903. Other aviators, or pilots, soon began to improve on the Wright brothers' plane design. These improvements allowed pilots to fly farther and achieve new milestones.

Throughout the 1920s, 117 American women became licensed pilots. These women competed in races and air shows. The most famous of these women was Amelia Earhart. Amelia was part of a team that flew across the Atlantic Ocean in 1928. In the late

Katherine Sui Fun Cheung immigrated to the United States from China in 1921. Her father was teaching her to drive a car near an airfield when she became interested in flying. In 1932, she began to take flying lessons. Soon after, she became the first Chinese American woman to earn a pilot's license. Cheung loved to perform aerobatics—airplane stunts—in air shows. She was also an early member of the Ninety-Nines.

1920s, she became a celebrity. She wrote a book, gave lectures, and even inspired a clothing line at Macy's, a department store. In 1932, she became the first woman to fly alone across the Atlantic Ocean.

In 1929, four female pilots, led by Fay Gillis, decided that they needed to form an organization. They sent a letter inviting all 117 licensed female pilots in the United States to meet up at a New York airfield. Their goals were simple: to meet other female pilots and to promote their success in aviation. They called themselves "the Ninety-Nines" because they had 99 original members. Amelia Earhart became the organization's first president.

The organization grew quickly, creating chapters throughout the United States. It sponsored air races and flying education. It was said that the Ninety-Nines "could find a friend in every airport." The Ninety-Nines also sponsored scholarships and museums to honor female pilots.

In the 1930s, strict safety rules for flying made it difficult for women to participate in air shows. Many began to work as flying instructors instead. Once World War II began in 1939, female pilots became involved in the war effort. Women were not allowed in combat at this time. Instead, female fliers contributed by training male pilots.

THE WOMEN'S AIR DERBY

In the 1920s, women were not allowed to compete against men in air races. Some races created a separate women's event so they could compete. The Women's Air Derby, part of the National Air Races of 1929, was one such event. It was here that the idea for the Ninety-Nines was born.

Secretary of Labor Frances Perkins

First Woman Cabinet Member: 1933

One day in 1911, Frances Perkins was having tea with family friends in New York City. The gathering heard a commotion and rushed outside. Down the street, the fire at the Triangle Shirtwaist Factory raged (page 7). Perkins witnessed the workers jumping to their deaths.

Perkins had already been working to end child labor. But seeing the horrible fire made her want to try even harder to help workers. She worked with the state's Committee on Safety to investigate the fire. With Perkins's input, the committee passed 36 new laws to protect workers.

In the 1920s, Perkins worked with New York governors Al Smith and Franklin D. Roosevelt. As the chairperson for the Industrial Commission, she used a logical approach to solve problems. Perkins directed questions about the issue to a group of experts. She then researched the problem before proposing a solution. Because of this, both governors trusted her to do quality work.

In 1933, when Franklin D. Roosevelt became president, he chose Perkins as part of his cabinet. The president's cabinet is a group of people who

give advice on how to run the country. Each cabinet member also has a government department to oversee. Perkins was the first woman ever to be part of a president's cabinet. As secretary of labor, she helped workers throughout the country.

During her time in the president's cabinet, Perkins helped pass many new laws to protect laborers. The two most important were the National Labor Relations Act (NLRA) and the Social Security Act. The NLRA made sure that workers could be part of unions. The Social Security Act provided a permanent system to help specific groups of needy people.

THE SOCIAL SECURITY ACT OF 1935

One of Frances Perkins's most important achievements was writing the Social Security Act. This set up a national government program of "social insurance" for Americans. The government takes a small percentage of workers' pay each month. This money is then used to help widows, orphans, and people who are unemployed, disabled, or retired.

Mary McLeod Bethune

The National Council of Negro Women: 1935

Knowing a little history from the 1800s helps us understand some of the problems Black people faced in the early 1900s. After the Civil War, the 13th Amendment ended slavery in 1864. The 15th Amendment gave formerly enslaved men the right to vote in 1870. But these changes to the Constitution could not immediately change racist attitudes. Southerners found ways to get around the new amendments and continued to discriminate against Black people.

Some Southerners began requiring that people pass a test or pay a tax in order to vote. Most Black

Ida B. Wells-Barnett is best remembered for her journalism. In the South, white mobs sometimes formed to attack and kill a Black man by hanging. This practice was called lynching. Wells-Barnett wrote a pamphlet and newspaper articles to expose the horrors of lynching. As a founder of the National Association of Colored Women's Clubs, she worked to promote voting rights for Black people and women. Wells-Barnett also supported Black workers' organizations in the 1920s.

people could not read or could not afford to pay, so these restrictions kept them from voting.

Southern states also passed laws to segregate Black and white people. Black people had to sit in different areas in public places, use separate bathrooms and water fountains, and go to separate schools. The Black facilities were usually very dirty and run-down. None of this officially violated the Constitution, so the states were allowed to do such things until the 1960s.

Mary McLeod Bethune grew up experiencing all of the problems Black people faced in the South. Women's issues and Black Americans' issues were not separate, even though they had sometimes been treated that way. Bethune worked for both causes, addressing both women's rights and civil rights for Black people. She founded the National Council of Negro Women in 1935. The council brought together 29 religious, political, and professional groups for Black women from around the country.

Bethune continued to work with many organizations to promote better lives for all Black people. In 1936, Bethune was named the director of the National Youth Administration's Division of Negro Affairs. This made her the highest-ranking Black woman in government. She also served as an advisor to President Roosevelt. Later, she would become president of the National Association for the Advancement of Colored People, the most important civil rights organization in the country.

LADIES LULAC

The League of United Latin American Citizens (LULAC) was founded in 1929. It was the first nationwide organization for Latinx rights. In 1933, Ladies LULAC was formed to organize female members. The group worked to promote the acceptance of Mexican American students in public schools and to assist Latinx citizens in voting.

CHAPTER THREE

1941 TO 1960

World War II began in Europe in 1939. On one side were the Allies: England, France, and the Soviet Union. They fought against the Axis powers: Germany, Italy, and Japan. The war began because the Axis countries had been invading and taking over other countries.

The Allies declared war on the Axis powers to try to stop them.

Like World War I, this war created a need for weapons and supplies. American factories began to manufacture these supplies. This created jobs for workers and helped the economy. The Great Depression finally ended.

When the war began, the United States said it was neutral, or not taking sides. Then, in 1941, Japan attacked the US military base at Pearl Harbor in Hawaii. As a result, American troops were sent to fight alongside other Allied troops in Europe, North Africa, and the Pacific Ocean. All of the Axis powers were defeated by August 1945.

After the war, the US economy continued to do well. American soldiers came home from the war. Many of these **veterans** were ready to get married and start families. This led to a baby boom, a time period when many more babies than usual were born. The late 1940s and 1950s became a time of prosperity and the promotion of family values.

Women working on a B-17 bomber in 1942

Rosie the Riveter: 1942

When World War II began in 1939, many people were
still suffering from the Great Depression. Because
the war created a demand for war supplies, many
Americans—mostly men at first—were eager to work
in defense factories. When women worked outside the
home, they usually had "women's jobs." These types
of jobs included teaching, nursing, or typing. Poorer
women might work in clothing factories or as maids
or nannies. But once the United States joined the war,
many men were needed for the military.

Factory workers were still needed, though. The government began to make propaganda that asked women to take jobs in factories that made **munitions**. Propaganda is advertising that usually attempts to use a person's emotions instead of reason to encourage them to do or buy something.

The government propaganda that enticed women to work in factories

used patriotic symbols to stir up emotions. The most famous example of this ad campaign is the "We Can Do It!" poster. It shows a female factory worker wearing denim work clothes and a red headscarf with polka dots. Her sleeve is rolled up, and she is flexing her bicep.

In 1943, a song came out called "Rosie the Riveter." The lyrics went like this: "All the day long, whether rain or shine, she's a part of the assembly line! She's making history, working for victory: Rosie the Riveter."

About five million American women entered the workforce during World War II. Many factories were only willing to hire white women. Companies who did hire Black women paid them less than white women were paid or only allowed the women to work as janitors.

Many people are familiar with the "We Can Do It!" poster today, but it was posted in factories for only two weeks during World War II. The image became popular in the 1980s as a symbol of women's empowerment.

JAPANESE INTERNMENT CAMPS

From 1942 to 1945, about 117,000 Japanese Americans were forced to live in crowded **concentration camps**, or internment camps. More than half of them were American citizens. President Roosevelt ordered this to prevent them from spying for the Japanese, one of America's enemies in World War II. In 1980, a government commission found that there had been very little threat from Japanese Americans. The camps were a product of racism.

Marie Wegman and umpire in 1948

The All-American Girls Professional Baseball League: 1943

The first official American baseball game was played in 1846, and the National Association of Professional Base Ball Players was established in 1871. By the 1920s, baseball had become very popular. Cities built ballparks especially for baseball games. Newspapers began to publish sports pages. Radio broadcasts of baseball games drew thousands of listeners. During the Great Depression, fewer people were able to attend games. But by the end of the 1930s, attendance was up again.

Once the United States entered World War II, there were fewer young men available to play baseball. Philip K. Wrigley, the owner of the Chicago Cubs, asked a committee to find a solution. The committee suggested that women play baseball instead. The All-American Girls Professional Baseball League was born in 1943.

Recruiters were sent out to find young women to play. Two hundred eighty women came to Chicago to try out, and 60 women were selected for the new league. They formed four teams of 15 women each. Each team had a famous male sports figure as a coach and a female chaperone.

The players trained hard so that the games could be competitive. They were also highly paid for the time period. Some players made more money than their parents did! The teams were very popular, and attendance for the games was high.

Before the war, it might have been difficult for people to accept women playing professional sports. That was something that men usually did. But now women were working in factories instead of men. The players were also required to wear feminine uniforms, makeup, and hairstyles. This may have helped ease the reception of the female ballplayers. The games continued to grow in popularity. By 1948, 10 teams were playing for 910,000 fans. But once the war ended, men's major-league baseball teams began to play again. Their games were shown on television. The new women's league became less popular and played its final season in 1954. Since then, women have been expected to play softball, not baseball.

HELENA RUBINSTEIN'S CHARM SCHOOL

The "girls" in the league were required to appear feminine and attractive at all times. To help them with this, they attended Helena Rubinstein's charm school. Players were required to carry a beauty kit with them. An official manual outlined a strict set of rules for their clothing and hygiene routines.

Eleanor Roosevelt holding the Universal Declaration of Human Rights in 1949

The Universal Declaration of Human Rights: 1948

Eleanor Roosevelt served as First Lady of the United States for 12 years. Many First Ladies who came before her served mainly as social hostesses for the president. But Mrs. Roosevelt wanted to take a more active role.

Because President Roosevelt was disabled, Mrs. Roosevelt often toured the country for him. She would talk to citizens and find out what their problems and concerns were. Much of President Roosevelt's time in office was during the Great Depression. Many people had problems with homelessness and poverty. In her travels, Mrs. Roosevelt also saw injured soldiers and victims of **genocide**. These experiences made her especially interested in helping children, women, and **minorities**.

After President Roosevelt died in 1945, President Harry Truman took office. Mrs. Roosevelt still wanted to be involved in politics, so President Truman appointed her as an **ambassador** to the United Nations (UN) in 1945. This was a new world organization formed after World War II. Its goal was to prevent war by encouraging countries to cooperate. Mrs. Roosevelt was the head of the committee that wrote the Universal Declaration of Human Rights. This declaration was a list of rights that all people deserved to have. The idea was that if all people felt respected and had their basic needs met, then they would be less likely to fight.

MEET THE OTHER WOMEN WHO WORKED ON THE UNIVERSAL DECLARATION OF HUMAN RIGHTS

Eleanor Roosevelt wasn't the only woman who contributed to the Universal Declaration of Human Rights. Originally the declaration read, "All men are born free and equal." Hansa Mehta, from India, suggested changing "men" to "human beings." Another female delegate was Begum Shaista Ikramullah from Pakistan. She wanted to be sure equal rights in marriage were included. Minerva Bernardino was a **feminist** from the Dominican Republic. She spoke up to ensure that women were covered throughout the document.

The declaration was adopted by the UN on December 10, 1948. This day is now known internationally as Human Rights Day. Mrs. Roosevelt summarized the declaration's purpose that day in a speech: "to lift [people] everywhere to a higher standard of life and to a greater enjoyment of freedom." The declaration serves as a list of principles for countries to follow. It has also contributed to other human rights agreements that have allowed women around the world to gain more rights and equality. One example of such an agreement is the Convention on the Elimination of All Forms of Discrimination against Women, which 64 countries signed in 1980.

THE RIGHTS IN THE UNIVERSAL DECLARATION

There are 30 articles in the Universal Declaration of Human Rights. Here are some highlights: All human beings are free and equal. Race, color, sex, religion, wealth, or politics shouldn't take away anyone's rights. Everyone has the right to life, freedom, and safety. Slavery, torture, and cruelty are wrong. Marriage should be based on consent. You can read all the articles at UN.org/en/about-us/universal-declaration -of-human-rights.

Four women service members in 1948

The Women's Armed Services Integration Act: 1948

During World War I, women served as nurses or did office work, but they were not officially considered part of the military. They had to get their own food and find their own places to stay. When the war was over, they did not get help from the government if they were injured. These were all things that male veterans received for their service.

At first, when the United States entered World War II, Congress created the Women's Army Auxiliary

Carmen Contreras-Bozak was the first Latina to serve in the Woman's Army Auxiliary Corps (WAAC). She was also the first of about 200 Puerto Rican women to do so. The army had been looking for bilingual women to work in communications. Contreras-Bozak volunteered to be part of the first WAAC unit to go overseas to North Africa. There, she sent coded messages from General Eisenhower's headquarters to the battlefield, earning the rank of technical sergeant.

Corps (WAAC). An auxiliary is a unit that works along with the military but is not a part of it. This provided the women with food, uniforms, places to stay, pay, and health care. But they weren't paid the same as men, and they didn't receive any of the other benefits that men got. In 1943, the WAAC was converted to the Women's Army Corps (WAC). This meant that women would temporarily be part of the actual army and could receive the same benefits that men could.

Women in the WAC were not allowed to join in the fighting. But they could do all sorts of other jobs that would free up men to fight. They drove supply trucks or worked as mechanics. Some were file clerks or typists. Others forecasted the weather, operated radios, or worked as code breakers. Still others worked as medical and dental technicians or as lab technicians.

The WAC was scheduled to expire in 1948. Before that happened, Congress passed a bill to make women a permanent part of the military. President Truman signed the Women's Armed Services Integration Act on June 12, 1948. This law made women a permanent part of the army, navy, marine corps, and air force. It did limit them to 2 percent of each branch at the time, though as of 2018, women made up approximately 17 percent of the armed forces. The navy and the air force have the largest percentages of female service members.

ALASKA TERRITORIAL GUARD

During World War II, Alaska was a territory of the United States. Alaska is located on the Pacific Ocean, far away from the US mainland, so it was open to attack. The government asked Alaskan natives to volunteer to protect their home. More than 27 Alaskan women served as part of the guard.

Lucille Ball and Vivian Vance, around 1951

Premier of *I Love Lucy*: 1951

Lucille "Lucy" Ball, an actor, started doing a radio comedy called *My Favorite Husband* in 1948. This show was very successful. In 1951, a TV company asked her to turn it into a TV show. Ball agreed—as long as her real-life husband, Desi Arnaz, could play the husband's role.

In the 1950s, almost all TV characters were white. But Arnaz was an immigrant from Cuba. The TV executives thought viewers would not believe that a white woman would be married to a Latino man. But Ball and Arnaz were able to convince them. *I Love Lucy* premiered on television in 1951. It was an immediate success! It continued to get high ratings for all six years it ran on television.

Most TV shows in that time were very true to 1950s ideas about how women and men should behave. A father would go to work each day at an office. A wife would stay at home to take care of the kids and clean the house. The children would learn simple moral lessons.

But *I Love Lucy* was different. Ricky, the husband, was a Cuban band leader who worked in a nightclub. Lucy, the wife, wanted to escape housework and get into showbiz, too. Lucy spent much of her time with her best friend, Ethel.

MEET PHYLLIS DILLER

Phyllis Diller was a stand-up comedian, actor, and author. Like Lucille Ball, she rebelled against 1950s **gender** roles. Many of her stand-up comedy routines involved making fun of her lack of abilities as a housewife. She wrote sarcastic books with titles like *Phyllis Diller's Housekeeping Hints* and *Phyllis Diller's Marriage Manual*. Diller also made jokes about her appearance. This was considered outrageous in a time when female role models were expected to be always perfectly groomed and graceful.

Lucy and Ethel were constantly scheming to find ways to have fun or get famous. They rebelled against ideas about how women were "supposed" to act.

Meanwhile, Ball herself was doing the same thing in real life. She was the first woman to head a TV production company. *I Love Lucy* also popularized new ways of making television comedies. The show was filmed in front of a live audience, had its own sets, and was the first to show reruns. Ball paved the way for women, like Queen Latifah, Eva Longoria, Reese Witherspoon, and Shonda Rhimes, to head their own production companies.

"GIRL GROUPS"

Rock and roll became popular with teenagers in the early 1950s. The first rock stars—Little Richard, Chuck Berry, and Elvis Presley—were men. But soon "girl groups" came on the scene. They usually sang harmonic songs with lyrics oriented toward innocent romance. Popular girl groups included the Shirelles, Martha and the Vandellas, and the Supremes.

Rosa Parks having her fingerprints taken in 1955

Rosa Parks Refuses to Give Up Her Seat: 1955

After the 13th Amendment ended slavery in 1865, the military occupied the South during a time called Reconstruction to make sure that the Southern states freed enslaved people and allowed them to vote. But as soon as the military left in 1877, Southern states passed laws, called Jim Crow laws, that segregated Black and white people. This meant Black and white people had to stay separate from each other in public places. For more than 75 years, discrimination and racism ruled the South, until the civil rights movement of the 1950s and 1960s.

Rosa Parks was a 42-year-old seamstress who worked at a local department store in Montgomery,

Felicitas Méndez was a California farm owner from Puerto Rico. Her children were not allowed to enroll at a whites-only school in Westminster, California, in 1944. The district sent them to a segregated "Mexican" school. Méndez and her husband, Gonzalo, organized Latinx families to sue the district for discrimination. In 1947, a federal court ruled that this segregation was against the Constitution. Latinx students were allowed to attend the same schools as white students.

Alabama. At the end of her workday on December 1, 1955, Parks boarded a city bus. City laws reserved the front halves of city buses for white people and the back halves for Black people. Parks sat in the first row of the Black section. Later during the bus ride, the white section filled up. A white man got on the bus, but there wasn't an available seat in the white section. The bus driver asked Parks to leave her seat. She did not, so the driver had her arrested.

Parks later explained that she wasn't physically too tired to stand. She wasn't too old to stand. She was just "tired of giving in."

Her actions led to the formation of the Montgomery Improvement Association, which was headed by

Martin Luther King Jr. The association worked with the Women's Political Council of Montgomery to organize a **boycott**. A boycott is the refusal by a large group of protestors to buy a product or service. This causes the company that sells the product or service to lose money. About 40,000 Black people boycotted the Montgomery bus system. Instead of riding the bus, they walked, cycled, took taxis, or gave each other rides to work.

The Montgomery bus boycott lasted for 381 days. Finally, after the Supreme Court ordered it, Montgomery's buses ended their policy of segregation on December 21, 1956. This was the first major event of the civil rights movement, which would continue through the 1950s and into the 1960s.

THE WOMEN'S POLITICAL COUNCIL

The Women's Political Council (WPC) of Montgomery, Alabama, was organized in 1949 to protest racist policies and help Black citizens vote. The WPC had been planning a bus boycott since 1953. Rosa Parks's arrest gave the organization the opportunity it had been looking for. The WPC was able to get the boycott underway by the time Parks was released from jail.

CHAPTER FOUR

1961
TO
1980

For about 15 years after World War II, much of American society was very prosperous. People were relieved that the war was over. Americans enjoyed being able to buy things like cars and televisions. Many veterans got married and started families. This was a period of

conservatism, when people just wanted to keep things the way they were.

But there were real social problems in America. Women and people of color were still being discriminated against. Many people were still poor. Black Americans began to organize to protest this treatment in the civil rights movement. This movement began in the 1950s and continued into the 1960s.

Two **liberal** presidents, John F. Kennedy and Lyndon B. Johnson, were in office for most of the 1960s. Liberal politicians want to make changes to the way things work. Some of the changes they tried to make in the 1960s had to do with more equality for Black people, women, and poor people.

In the late 1960s and early 1970s, other groups were inspired by the way Black Americans had stood up for their rights in the civil rights movement. Women, Latinx, and Indigenous and LGBTQ people all began to fight to gain equal treatment as well.

The cover of *Silent Spring*

Silent Spring Is Published: 1962

Historically, it was hard to be a female scientist. In the early 20th century, women who wanted to study to be scientists were usually only allowed to attend women's colleges. When they graduated, they often were able to work only as a male scientist's assistant. Science magazines almost never talked about the work of female scientists. Many times, women who worked on a research project were not even listed on the research report.

In spite of these challenges, Rachel Carson managed to become a marine biologist, a scientist who studies life in bodies of water. In 1936, Carson became the second woman ever hired by the US Bureau of Fisheries.

Carson was working at the bureau when she noticed that the use of pesticides—sprays that protect crops from insects—was hurting fish and other animals. One pesticide in particular, called DDT, was especially deadly to birds. She began to do more research on the effects of these pesticides. Carson learned that they were also hurting humans and the environment.

MEET GRACE HOPPER

Grace Hopper was an early computer engineer and programmer. She earned her PhD in mathematics from Yale in 1934. In the 1940s, she worked on the teams that produced the Mark I and UNIVAC I, two early computers. Early computer programmers used long strings of numbers or mathematical equations to "talk" to the machines. Hopper developed the first English-like computer processing language, called FLOW-MATIC. Because of it, later computer languages were more user-friendly.

In 1962, Carson published her findings in the book *Silent Spring*. The title referred to how spring would sound if pesticides killed off many birds and other creatures. In the book, Carson made the argument that humans must start using chemicals more responsibly. If they did not, there would be terrible consequences for the environment.

The book had a huge impact. Carson appeared on a special television program and testified before Congress. Most important, the government created the Environmental Protection Agency in 1970. This agency eventually banned the use of DDT. The popularity of the book also led to the growth of the modern environmental movement. Every time you recycle something, remember to conserve water, or celebrate Earth Day, you're paying a little tribute to Rachel Carson!

EARTH DAY

The first Earth Day took place on April 22, 1970. By then, *Silent Spring* had raised public awareness of pollution and its effects on the environment. Twenty million Americans joined in protests and rallies to draw attention to the need to take action. Earth Day became an international event in 1990 and celebrated its 50th anniversary in 2020.

Congresswoman Shirley Chisholm in 1972

Equality Under the Law: 1963 to 1972

In 1961, President John F. Kennedy set up a commission, or a group of advisors, to look into how women were being treated in schools and at work. The group reported that women faced discrimination in many workplaces in America. For example, in 1960, women were paid about one-third less than men who did the same work.

The commission's report led to the passage of the Equal Pay Act in 1963. This act requires employers to pay men and women who are doing the same job the same amount of money. This was one of the

Shirley Chisholm became the first Black woman elected to Congress in 1968. She introduced more than 50 bills that would help the poor or promote equality. In 1970, to encourage the passage of the ERA, she spoke to Congress: "The Constitution they wrote was designed to protect the rights of white male citizens, as there were no Black Founding Fathers, there were no founding mothers—a great pity, on both counts."

first national laws that specifically targeted discrimination against working women.

In 1964, President Lyndon B. Johnson signed the Civil Rights Act of 1964 into law. This made it illegal to discriminate against anyone due to their race, sex, religion, color, or nationality. Now women were protected by federal law from any kind of discrimination.

A national law protecting people from discrimination is a powerful thing. But an amendment to the Constitution is stronger! It is much, much harder to get rid of an amendment than a law. We read in chapter 2 that the National Women's Party and Daniel Anthony Jr. first presented the Equal Rights Amendment (ERA) to Congress in 1923 (page 29), but it failed to pass.

After the success of the Equal Pay Act and the Civil Rights Act of 1964, activists became hopeful again for the amendment's passage.

Representative Martha Griffiths reintroduced the ERA to Congress in 1971. Both houses approved it! All that was needed was for 38 states to ratify it by 1982, and it could be added to the Constitution. But only 35 states ratified it.

Still, many people fought for the ERA. A new movement for getting it ratified began in 2011, but in 2020 the government decided that too much time had passed. The resolution is no longer up for ratification.

STOP ERA

STOP ERA, founded by Phyllis Schlafly in 1972, opposed the Equal Rights Amendment. The group feared its passage would require women to fight in wars or force men and women to use the same public restrooms. Another worry was that divorced fathers might not be required to pay child support anymore.

Betty Friedan talking to reporters in 1967

CIVIL RIGHTS FOR WOMEN

The National Organization for Women: 1966

Just after World War II, a baby boom began. There was a rise in the birth rate—the number of babies being born. Expectations for women in their roles as mothers were very high. The "ideal" wife and mother shown on television did not work outside the home. She was beautifully dressed and obeyed her husband. She kept her house perfectly clean and took excellent care of her children. She was happy to spend her days vacuuming, cooking, and supervising children at play.

Some women did not like these expectations. One of these women, Betty Friedan, wrote a book called

The Feminine Mystique in 1963. In the book, Friedan argued that being a suburban mother was boring and lonely. She thought that if women could work outside the home, they would feel better.

Friedan was only thinking about wealthier white women. Many poorer women already did work outside the home—about 40 percent! They did jobs that were considered "women's work." Some of these jobs included teaching, nursing, childcare, telephone operations, housecleaning, and secretarial work.

MEET AILEEN CLARKE HERNANDEZ

Aileen Clarke Hernandez was a co-founder of the National Organization of Women (NOW) and served as its second national president from 1970 to 1971. Previously, Hernandez had been the only woman on President Johnson's Equal Employment Opportunity Commission. This commission was established to enforce the Civil Rights Act of 1964. She was involved with many other organizations that promoted social justice over the years. In honor of her work, she was nominated for a Nobel Peace Prize in 2005.

Nonetheless, some middle-class white women loved Friedan's book. They had noticed the success of the Black civil rights movement. Additionally, there was now legal support for women's equality with the Equal Pay and Civil Rights acts. These women thought that they, too, might be able to protest and gain more freedom for themselves.

Betty Friedan, Kathryn Clarenbach, and Aileen Hernandez founded the National Organization for Women (NOW) in 1966. Its original goals were to help women fully participate in American society and enjoy the same privileges and responsibilities as men. NOW is still active and cites its current core issues on its website. These include ending violence against women, promoting racial justice, and supporting the ERA.

THE 1969 STONEWALL RIOTS

In 1969 in New York City, LGBTQ people began demonstrating against **homophobia**, or anti-gay sentiment and violence. A single protest turned into a movement for equality for LGBTQ people. Marsha P. Johnson, a **transgender** woman, was a pioneer in the LGBTQ liberation movement in the United States.

Gloria Steinem speaking at the United Nations in 1978

Ms. Magazine: 1971

Gloria Steinem began her career as a writer and feminist activist. A feminist is someone who believes that women and men should be treated equally. Steinem spoke to Congress in favor of the Equal Rights Amendment in 1970. To promote the amendment, she wrote an article for *Time* magazine about what life would be like if women and men were truly equal. Steinem also helped found the National Women's Political Caucus in 1971. This group supports women who want to work in government.

Steinem is most famous for her work with *Ms.* magazine. Steinem and Dorothy Pitman Hughes

Dorothy Pitman Hughes was running a multiracial day care center in New York City when she met Gloria Steinem. Hughes and Steinem co-founded *Ms.* magazine together. They also co-founded the Women's Action Alliance, which promoted equality in education. Hughes set up New York City's first shelter for women who had suffered abuse. Later, in Jacksonville, Florida, she fought poverty with a community gardening program.

wanted to publish a magazine that was written by women, for women. They noticed that most magazines aimed toward women were about things like housekeeping and fashion. Steinem and Hughes hoped to write about real women fighting to be treated equally.

The first issue of *Ms.* showed an eight-armed woman juggling items associated with her home and her career. One article discussed how living on government welfare affected women. Another explained the 1972 presidential candidates' stances on women's issues.

A third article covered bias against women in the English language. For example, why not use the word "humankind" instead of "mankind"? Other words mentioned were "policeman" and "stewardess." The authors suggested replacing them with "police officer" and "flight attendant." In fact, the very title of the magazine reflects this topic. Unlike "Miss" or "Mrs.," "Ms." is a title that a woman can use that does not reveal whether she is married.

According to its website, *Ms.* was "the first national magazine to make . . . a feminist worldview available to the public." The magazine is still doing that 50 years later!

WOMAN ALIVE!

From 1974 to 1977, *Ms.* magazine had its own television series. The series was called *Woman Alive!* It included short documentaries that gave information about famous feminists. Other episodes were about the lives of ordinary women or problems like job discrimination.

Billie Jean King wins the Women's Singles final in 1978

The Battle of the Sexes: 1973

Billie Jean King began playing tennis at a young age. She was also young when she realized that female tennis players were treated differently than male tennis players. When she was 12, she was not allowed to be in a group picture at her tennis club because she was wearing shorts instead of a tennis skirt.

King worked hard and turned out to be great at tennis. She was the top-ranking woman in the world in tennis for six separate years in the late 1960s and early 1970s. King also won many championship titles that came with prize money. But there was a problem—women were always awarded less prize money than men were. King became the first president of the Women's Tennis Association. This group fought to get equal amounts of prize money for women and men at tennis tournaments. It succeeded! In 1973, the US Open tournament announced that it would offer equal prizes to women and men.

MEET WILMA RUDOLPH

Wilma Rudolph was one of 22 children. As a young girl, she contracted both scarlet fever and polio, a crippling disease. The doctor told her she would never walk again. But at age 16, Rudolph won a bronze track-and-field medal in the 1956 Olympics. In the 1960 Olympics, she won three gold medals and broke three world records! The very next year, Rudolph was named Associated Press Female Athlete of the Year.

Later that year, a former male tennis champion, Bobby Riggs, began claiming that women's tennis was not as good as men's tennis. He bragged that even a 55-year-old such as himself could beat one of the top women players. King was 29 and at the top of her game. She accepted his challenge. She said, "I'm taking this match very seriously … I welcome the responsibility and the pressure."

To make the match more exciting, television promoters decided to call it the "Battle of the Sexes." It was broadcast on September 20, 1973, to about 90 million viewers. It was the most watched tennis match of all time! Of course, King won. Thanks to her win, as well as Title IX, girls and women were encouraged to participate more freely in sports.

TITLE IX

Title IX was part of a federal law passed in 1972. Title IX made it illegal for any school that received money from the national government to discriminate against someone based on their sex. This law resulted in a big increase in sports programs for girls in public schools.

Coretta Scott King speaking in support of feminism in 1977

The Combahee River Collective: 1974

Many of the leaders of the women's rights movement of the 1970s were middle-class white women. In 1974, 90 percent of the members of the National Organization for Women were white. The problems that these white women faced were very different from those faced by many Black women.

Black women were much more likely to be poor than white women were. They were also much more likely to work outside the home to support their families, not because they wanted to be fulfilled by a career. Women of color were more frequently single parents. They also faced racism in addition to sexism.

MEET MARTHA P. COTERA

Martha P. Cotera is an author, **Chicano** civil rights activist, and Chicana feminist. Cotera was very active in Texas politics in the 1970s. But it is her work as a historian that has been most significant. Many historians argued that there was simply very little information about women of Hispanic descent to study. In 1976, Cotera published a complete history of Latina women from before Columbus arrived to the present day.

This is an example of a concept called **intersectionality**. It means that people have many characteristics that make up their identities. The way these characteristics combine, or intersect, affects the way each person is treated by society. For example, you probably have several identities. You have a racial and ethnic identity: Black, white, Latinx, Indigenous, Asian, and so on. You have a gender identity: female, male, or **non-binary**. You have identities based on physical traits: tall, short, curly-haired, straight-haired, and so on. You have a **socioeconomic** identity: working-class, middle-class, or upper-class. Essentially, you belong to a lot of groups! The specific combination of groups you belong to contributes to the privileges or challenges that you face in the world.

In 1974, a group of Black feminists formed the Combahee River Collective. They were led by Barbara Smith, Beverly Smith, Demita Frazier, and Audre Lorde. The group's name honored the Combahee River Raid. During this 1863 raid, Harriet Tubman freed hundreds of enslaved people. The women who formed the Combahee River Collective wanted to create an organization that focused on the combination of racism, sexism, and homophobia, or anti-gay sentiment, that they faced. In 1977, they released the Combahee River Collective Statement, which explained these goals.

Though the collective disbanded in 1980, it was groundbreaking in pointing out the importance of intersectionality.

WOMEN OF ALL RED NATIONS

In Rapid City, South Dakota, in 1974, Lorelei DeCora Means, Madonna Thunder Hawk, Phyllis Young, and Janet McCloud came together with a group of women to form Women of All Red Nations. This group wanted to focus on issues that were problems for Indigenous people, many of whom lived on reservations. Some of these problems were high poverty and poor education. They also sought to address specific issues of Indigenous women's health.

CHAPTER FIVE

1981 TO 2000

Women's rights activists accomplished many things in the 1960s and 1970s. Legal protections for women increased. The Equal Pay Act, the Civil Rights Act of 1964, and Title IX protected women from some types of discrimination. Feminists published books and magazines that became well known. This ensured that many Americans were familiar with their ideas about equality.

In the 1980s and 1990s, women began to enjoy the fruits of these activists' labors. More and more women appeared in public life. There were a lot of "first female this" and "first female that" in the 1980s and 1990s! Today, it doesn't seem like a big deal that a woman might be an astronaut, a senator, or a Supreme Court justice. That's thanks to the work of these trail-blazing women who made powerful women seem ordinary.

Justices Sandra Day O'Connor, Sonia Sotomayor, Ruth Bader Ginsburg, and Elena Kagan

First Female Supreme Court Justice: 1981

Sandra Day O'Connor began her career as a lawyer in 1952. In those days, it was hard for a female lawyer to find a job. She was offered a job as a legal secretary in San Mateo County, California. O'Connor preferred to work for free as a lawyer for several months to prove that a woman could do the job. Finally, she was given a paying job as deputy county attorney.

O'Connor then worked in other positions. She was an attorney for the US Army, an Arizona state senator, and an Arizona appellate court judge. Then, in 1981, President Ronald Reagan appointed her to the Supreme Court. She was the first female Supreme Court justice ever.

Supreme Court justices have a lot of influence over the law because they can decide whether the laws that

Congress has made are **constitutional**. If a law does not go along with something that is written in the Constitution, the Supreme Court can **strike the law down**.

During her time on the Supreme Court, O'Connor voted to protect equal rights for men and women. She retired in 2006 to take care of her husband, who had become ill. Even after her retirement, O'Connor continued to have an influence. She founded a program called iCivics, an educational website for middle and high schoolers that promotes interesting ways of learning about government and politics.

The second woman appointed to the Supreme Court was Ruth Bader Ginsburg. Before her work on the Supreme Court, Ginsburg worked for the American Civil Liberties Union (ACLU). The ACLU is

MEET SONIA SOTOMAYOR

Sonia Sotomayor was the first person of Hispanic descent to serve as a Supreme Court justice. Both of her parents were native Puerto Ricans, though Sotomayor was born in the Bronx, New York. Sotomayor sat as a justice on two levels of federal courts before being appointed to the Supreme Court by President Obama in 2009. She tends to lean toward increased civil liberties, or personal freedoms, in her decisions.

an organization famous for helping people who have faced some kind of discrimination. In this job, Ginsburg argued six Supreme Court cases about gender equality.

After being appointed as a Supreme Court justice in 1993, Ginsburg was never afraid to voice her opinion. When a justice does not agree with the ruling of the majority of the Supreme Court, they write what is called a dissenting opinion. This is an explanation of why they disagree. Ginsburg wrote many dissenting opinions during her time on the Supreme Court. In 2013, a law school student gave her the nickname "Notorious RBG," and Ginsburg became an icon for girls and women who don't always agree with the way things are.

MISSISSIPPI UNIVERSITY FOR WOMEN V. HOGAN

Mississippi University for Women v. Hogan was the first case that Sandra Day O'Connor heard as a Supreme Court justice. Joe Hogan, a nurse, had not been admitted to the nursing program at Mississippi University for Women because he was male. The Supreme Court ruled that this was discrimination and that Hogan should be allowed to attend the school. This was important because it showed that gender discrimination could work both ways.

Sally Ride floating on the space shuttle Challenger in 1983

Sally Ride Goes to Space: 1983

Sally Ride grew up loving science. Science toys, like her telescope and chemistry set, were some of her favorites. She was also an excellent athlete and enjoyed playing tennis. These childhood interests would come in handy when she traveled to space as an adult!

Ride trained to be a physicist at Stanford University. She was about to finish her doctoral degree when she saw an ad from the National Aeronautics and Space Administration (NASA). The ad said that NASA was looking for scientists and that women were allowed to apply! Ride was one of only six women chosen in 1978.

During her training, Ride was a communications officer for two flights of the *Columbia* space shuttle. She also helped develop a robotic arm that could be used to move objects around in space.

Finally, Ride was ready to be assigned to an actual space mission. In 1983, she became the first American woman in space and the youngest American in space to date. She made two space missions, both aboard the space shuttle *Challenger*.

In 1987, Ride retired from NASA and began working for Stanford University and the University of California. She believed strongly that basic science education in public schools needed to be improved. To promote science education, she wrote seven children's science books. Ride also directed several space education programs for middle schoolers. She co-founded Sally Ride Science, a program to help science, technology, engineering, and mathematics (STEM) students and teachers. These types of STEM programs are very popular in schools today.

Ride won so many awards that it is hard to list them all. One of the most important was the Presidential Medal of Freedom. She was also inducted into the National Women's Hall of Fame.

THE *CHALLENGER* DISASTER

On January 28, 1986, thousands of American schoolchildren watched the *Challenger* launch on television. It was the space shuttle's 10th mission, and Christa McAuliffe, a teacher from New Hampshire, was to be the first civilian in space. But 73 seconds after liftoff, the shuttle exploded into a fireball. The crew members on board died instantly. Engineers learned later that the cold temperatures that day had caused some of the rocket boosters to leak fuel, causing the explosion. To honor their memories, the families of the *Challenger* crew created a network of Challenger Learning Centers to promote learning about technology, engineering, and math.

Gerda Lerner

Women's History Month: 1987

It started with just one day: International Women's Day, celebrated on March 8. Labor activists in several countries started the tradition in the early 1900s. The first Women's Day was organized in New York in 1909. Others were held in Austria, Denmark, Germany, Switzerland, and the Soviet Union. After a while, it became a holiday in many countries.

In 1977, the United Nations proclaimed March 8 International Women's Day. If one day is good, why not a whole week? The next year, women got a week, at least in Sonoma School District in California. Then, in

1979, Sarah Lawrence College sponsored a conference about women's history. Participants at the conference heard about Sonoma's women's history week. They agreed to organize their own women's history weeks in their own communities. They promised to try to get a national women's history week set up.

President Jimmy Carter came through in 1980 with support for National Women's History Week. He wrote, "From the first settlers who came to our shores, from the first American Indian families who befriended them, men and women have worked together to build this nation. Too often the women were unsung and sometimes their contributions went unnoticed. But the achievements, leadership, courage, strength and love of the

MEET GERDA LERNER

Gerda Lerner was an Austrian Jewish woman who immigrated to the United States in 1939. Lerner became interested in women's history and completed a PhD in history at Columbia University in 1966. Lerner wrote numerous feminist histories and became the director of the women's history graduate program at Sarah Lawrence College. Lerner sponsored the 1979 women's history conference that got the ball rolling for Women's History Month.

women who built America was as vital as that of the men whose names we know so well."

If a week is good, well, why not a month? Fourteen states had decided that was a great idea by 1986. Congress agreed in 1987 by passing a resolution. Now thousands of schools across the nation celebrate women every March.

NATIONAL WOMEN'S HISTORY PROJECT

The National Women's History Project began in 1980 to persuade Congress to officially make March Women's History Month. In 2018, the organization changed its name to National Women's History Alliance. The alliance names a theme for every year's celebration and works to support the study of women's history all year long.

Female US senators in 1997

The Year of the Woman: 1992

In 1991, a special trial was held in the Senate. When these trials happen, the Senate Judiciary Committee asks witnesses questions. One of these witnesses was a woman. Though there were two women in the Senate, there were no women on the Judiciary Committee. All the senators questioning the witness were men.

Many people watched this trial on television. Several women saw male senators ask the witness questions they thought were insulting. They saw that the female witness was very uncomfortable. They thought there should be more women in the

Senate. Maybe then women could be better represented on the Judiciary Committee, too.

That is how four women were inspired to run for Senate in 1992. One was Patty Murray, a Washington state senator at the time. Another was Dianne Feinstein, who had been the mayor of San Francisco and had unsuccessfully run to be the governor of California. A third was Barbara Boxer, a former stockbroker who was representing California in the House of Representatives. Finally, there was Carol Moseley Braun, who had been part of the Illinois state legislature and would be the first Black female senator.

Spoiler alert: All four of these women were elected to the Senate! They joined the two women already there—Nancy L. Kassebaum of Kansas and Barbara

Mikulski of Maryland. The total number of women tripled! Newspapers and magazines called it the "Year of the Woman." Mikulski had a great response: "Calling 1992 the Year of the Woman makes it sound like the Year of the Caribou or the Year of the Asparagus. We're not a fad."

Mikulski was right: Women are not a fad! As of 2021, a total 58 women have served in the Senate, and 24 of those are currently serving.

SENATE PAGES

Senate pages were historically young boys who served as messengers and general helpers to senators. In 1971, Senator Fred Harris argued that girls should also be admitted to the page program. The Senate should "end discriminatory hiring practices based on sex alone," he urged, to "serve as an example [to] employers at all levels of American industry." Soon after in May 1971, the first three female pages—Paulette Desell, Ellen McConnell, and Julie Price—were sworn in.

Secretary of State Madeleine Albright in 1997

First Female Secretary of State: 1997

The secretary of state is one of the president's advisors. This advisor is also the main person who carries out the country's foreign policy—the relationship that the United States has with other countries.

In 1948, when she was 11 years old, Madeleine Albright immigrated to the United States from what is now the Czech Republic. She became a US citizen and earned her PhD in government at Columbia University. Early in her career, Albright worked in the White House as a staff member for President Jimmy Carter.

Later, she served as an ambassador to the United Nations.

In 1997, Albright became the first female secretary of state. She was appointed by President Bill Clinton. As secretary of state, Albright had to deal with several difficult situations in Europe. One problem was that many countries in Eastern Europe had recently become independent. This might not seem to be a problem, but previously, they had been part of the Soviet Union, an enemy of the United States. Albright worked to convince these countries to become allies, or friends, of the United States. She also tried to help them form democratic governments.

Another problem was in Kosovo, an area in southern Europe, a bit north of Greece. Three groups were fighting over territory. The United States was part of the North Atlantic Treaty Organization (NATO),

MEET AIDA ÁLVAREZ

Aida Álvarez started her career working as a journalist. She then became an investment banker. She also worked in the federal housing industry. In 1997, Álvarez was appointed by President Bill Clinton to head the Small Business Administration. This made her the first Latina woman to serve as a member of a president's cabinet.

a military alliance. Albright worked with NATO to help end the conflict in Kosovo.

Albright set the stage for other women to serve as secretary of state, too. Condoleezza Rice became the first Black female secretary of state in 2005. She worked for the George W. Bush administration. Hillary Clinton became secretary of state for the Barack Obama administration in 2009.

SPECIAL SUPPLEMENTAL NUTRITION PROGRAM FOR WOMEN, INFANTS, AND CHILDREN

The Special Supplemental Nutrition Program for Women, Infants, and Children, known as WIC, is a program that is part of the US Department of Agriculture, one of the agencies of the president's cabinet. The program provides healthcare, food, and nutrition information to pregnant women, breastfeeding mothers, new mothers, and children under the age of five.

Brandi Chastain celebrating her winning penalty kick

The FIFA Women's World Cup: 1999

The first FIFA Women's World Cup tournament was held in 1991 in China. Twelve teams competed, and the United States won. The next tournament, held in 1995, resulted in a win for Norway.

The third tournament, hosted in 1999, was historic for female athletics for several reasons. The tournament, which consisted of 32 games, was held in the United States for the first time. It was the first time the games were played in huge stadiums. About 40 million Americans watched the 32 games of the tournament on live television.

The final game broke a women's sporting attendance record. Some 90,000 spectators attended the event at the Rose Bowl in Pasadena, California. China was playing against the United States. The United States, as the host nation, was eager to secure a victory on its home turf. But China was also eager to win, after having hosted the tournament and lost in 1991.

Important players for the United States included Mia Hamm, Brandi Chastain, Michelle Akers, and Kristine Lilly. Fan Yunjie, Liu Ying, Xie Huilin, and Sun Wen distinguished themselves on the Chinese team.

The game itself was fairly unexciting: No one had been able to score a goal until extra time, when the teams squared off for penalty kicks. A penalty kick is when a team member tries to kick the ball past the goalie of the other team.

After two hours of playing, including 30 minutes of extra time, Chastain, a defender for the US team, propelled the team's fifth penalty kick past China's goalkeeper. With one swift kick, the US team had won the championship.

The crowd roared with applause. Chastain, in an iconic moment of celebration, whipped off her jersey and waved it above her head. (She was wearing a sports bra underneath.) Some people were scandalized. Others considered it a feminist moment—no one would have been shocked had a man done the same thing! Regardless, the 1999 game launched a new era for women's soccer and was a milestone in the history of women's sports.

INTERNATIONAL WOMEN'S SPORTS HALL OF FAME

To recognize the achievements of women athletes and coaches, the International Women's Sports Hall of Fame was founded in 1980. It is part of the Women's Sports Foundation. Some of the awards that it issues are the Billie Jean King Leadership Award, the Wilma Rudolph Courage Award, the Champion for Equality Award, and the Sportswoman of the Year Award.

LOOKING AHEAD

Women have come a long way in 100 years! At the turn
of the 20th century, women could not vote in most
states or in federal elections. They were not allowed to
have certain jobs, could not attend many universities,
and were not given equal pay for equal work. Thanks
to the hard work of the activists we've read about—and
scores of others—modern women can appreciate far
more opportunities.

In the 21st century, women work in every field.
They are doctors, lawyers, mechanics, military
officers, business owners, astronauts, and athletes.
In the first 20 years of this century, women have
made even more strides in the field of politics.
Condoleezza Rice became the first Black female
secretary of state in 2005. Hillary Clinton was the
first female presidential candidate for a major
political party in 2016. Kamala Harris, a woman of

color, was elected as the first female vice president in 2020. Three more female Supreme Court justices were appointed: Sonia Sotomayor in 2009, Elena Kagan in 2010, and Amy Coney Barrett in 2020. The 177th Congress (2021–2022) included 145 female members—more than 25 percent women!

In spite of these accomplishments, society still has some work to do. As of 2020, women made 81 cents for every dollar that men made. Only 12 percent of American women have access to paid maternity leave. Seventy-seven percent of women now work outside the home, but they are still expected to handle the majority of childcare and housework.

The women of the 20th century who fought for the rights that modern women enjoy continue to inspire new generations to work toward equality.

GLOSSARY

activist: A person who believes in forceful action (like a mass demonstration) for political purposes

ambassador: A high-ranking person in government who represents their government in other countries

boycott: Refusal to deal with a person, store, or organization until certain conditions are met or agreed to

Chicano/Chicana: An American with Mexican ancestry

civil rights: Basic rights that every person has to be treated fairly and equally

concentration camp: A place where a large number of people are held by the government

conservatism: The belief that the current situation should not change

Constitution of the United States: A document written in 1787 right after the United States first became a country, which states the basic laws, instructions, and rules for how the country must be run

constitutional: In agreement with the ideas in the Constitution

credit: To purchase something now but pay for it later

economic: Having to do with money or the production, distribution, or selling of goods and services

federal: Having to do with the central or national government of the United States

feminist: A person who believes in and works toward the equality of the sexes

gender: The behavioral, cultural, or emotional traits typically associated with one sex

genocide: The purposeful destruction of a racial, political, or cultural group

homophobia: Discrimination against LGBTQ people

immigrant: A person born in one country who moves to another country and settles there

inauguration: A special ceremony that is held in January after a new US president is elected to officially mark the beginning of their presidency

Indigenous: The first group of people to live in a geographical location; sometimes called Native Americans or American Indians in the United States

industrialization: The use of factories to make goods

intersectionality: The way different forms of discrimination combine

Latinx: A person from Latin America

LGBTQ: Acronym for lesbian, gay, bisexual, transgender, and queer/questioning

liberal: Believing that the current situation should change

militant: Forceful in action

minority: A part of a population that differs in some way from other groups and is often given unfair treatment

munitions: Objects fired from guns or explosives that can be used in war, such as bullets or bombs

non-binary: People who do not feel like the word "girl" or "boy" fits them

people of color: Non-white people; can refer to Black people, Indigenous people, people of Asian descent, people of Hispanic descent, etc.

poverty: The state of being poor

prejudice: Favoring or disliking something without a good reason; unfriendly feelings directed against a person, group, or race

progressivism: The idea that people and the government should work together to solve problems in society

prosperity: Having enough money to buy everything one needs and many things one wants

segregate: To separate people, usually based on their race or skin color

socioeconomic: Relating to the classification of people according to how much wealth they have

strike: Refusing to work until demands are met

strike down (a law): The cancellation or removal of a law by the Supreme Court because it goes against the ideas of the Constitution

transgender: When a person's gender identity (how they feel: boy, girl, or non-binary) is different than what doctors assigned to them when they were born (girl or boy)

union: A group of workers who agree to work together to bargain with their bosses for better working conditions

urbanization: The movement of people from the country to cities

veteran: A person who has fought in a war

working-class: People who perform jobs that require little or no special skills

RESOURCES

Books

Clinton, Chelsea. *She Persisted: 13 American Women Who Changed the World.* New York: Philomel Books, 2017.

Ignotofsky, Rachel. *Women in Science: 50 Fearless Pioneers Who Changed the World.* New York: Ten Speed Press, 2016.

Levy, Debbie. *Becoming RBG: Ruth Bader Ginsburg's Journey to Justice.* New York: Simon & Schuster Books for Young Readers, 2019.

Skeers, Linda. *Women Who Dared: 52 Stories of Fearless Daredevils, Adventurers, and Rebels.* Naperville, IL: Sourcebooks, 2017.

Thimmesh, Catherine. *Madam President: The Extraordinary, True (and Evolving) Story of Women in Politics.* New York: Houghton Mifflin Harcourt, 2008.

Websites

A Mighty Girl: amightygirl.com

National Women's History Museum: womenshistory.org

Women and the American Story: wams.nyhistory.org

Women Heroes on National Geographic Kids: kids.national geographic.com/history/topic/women-heroes

Women's History for Kids on the National Park Service: nps.gov /subjects/womenshistory/for-kids.htm

SELECTED REFERENCES

Anderson, Karen Tucker. "Last Hired, First Fired: Black Women Workers during World War II." *Journal of American History* 69, no. 1 (1982): 82–97. doi.org/10.2307/1887753.

Bellafaire, Judith A. *The Women's Army Corps: A Commemoration of World War II Service.* US Army Center of Military History, 1993. History.Army.mil/brochures/WAC/WAC.HTM.

Brady, Kathleen. "Why We Still Love Lucy." PBS. October 2017. PBS .org/wgbh/americanexperience/features/why-we-still-love-lucy.

Brice, Anne. "The Montgomery Bus Boycott and the Women Who Made It Possible." *Berkeley News.* February 11, 2020. News.Berkeley.edu/2020/02/11/podcast-montgomery -bus-boycott-womens-political-council.

Diamond, Anna. "The True Story behind Billie Jean King's Victorious 'Battle of the Sexes.'" *Smithsonian.* September 22, 2017. SmithsonianMag.com/smithsonian-institution /true-story-behind-billie-jean-king-battle-sexes-180964985.

Gant, Kelli. "Women Involved in Aviation." Ninety-Nines. Accessed May 1, 2021. Ninety-Nines.org/women-in-aviation-article.htm.

Girl Scouts of America. "Our History: The Vision of Juliette Gordon Low." Accessed May 1, 2021. GirlScouts.org/en/about-girl -scouts/our-history.html.

History, Art & Archives. "Rankin, Jeannette." United States House of Representatives. Accessed May 1, 2021. History.House.gov /People/Listing/R/RANKIN,-Jeannette-(R000055)/.

ILR School. "The 1911 Triangle Factory Fire." Cornell University. Accessed May 1, 2021. TriangleFire.ILR.Cornell.edu.

Khan Academy. "American Women and World War II." Accessed May 1, 2021. KhanAcademy.org/humanities/us-history/rise-to -world-power/us-wwii/a/american-women-and-world-war-ii.

Law, Tara. "Virginia Just Became the 38th State to Pass the Equal Rights Amendment. Here's What to Know about the History of the ERA." *Time.* Last modified January 15, 2020. Time.com/5657997/equal-rights-amendment-history.

Little, Becky. "How Eleanor Roosevelt Pushed for a Universal Declaration of Human Rights." History. December 8, 2020. History.com/news/eleanor-roosevelt-universal-declaration -human-rights.

MacGregor, Molly Murphy. "Why March Is National Women's History Month." National Women's History Alliance. Accessed May 1, 2021. NationalWomensHistoryAlliance.org/womens -history-month/womens-history-month-history.

Napikoski, Linda. "Combahee River Collective in the 1970s." ThoughtCo. Last modified January 30, 2019. ThoughtCo.com /combahee-river-collective-information-3530569.

National Archives. "The 19th Amendment." Last modified May 14, 2020. Archives.gov/exhibits/featured-documents /amendment-19.

National Organization for Women. "Founding." Last modified July 2011. NOW.org/about/history/founding-2.

Office of the Historian. "Biographies of the Secretaries of State: Madeleine Korbel Albright." US Department of State. Accessed May 1, 2021. History.State.gov/departmenthistory/people /albright-madeleine-korbel.

Roosevelt, Eleanor. "Adoption of the Declaration of Human Rights." Speech to the General Assembly of the United Nations at Paris, France, December 1948. EdChange Multicultural Pavilion. EdChange.org/multicultural/speeches/eleanor_roosevelt _adoption.html.

Schuessler, Jennifer. "The Complex History of the Women's Suffrage Movement." *New York Times*. August 15, 2019. NYTimes.com /2019/08/15/arts/design/womens-suffrage-movement.html.

Silentology (blog). "The History (and Mythology) of 1920s Flapper Culture." March 1, 2018. Silentology.Wordpress.com/2018/03/01 /the-history-and-mythology-of-1920s-flapper-culture.

Thulin, Lila. "The 97-Year-History of the Equal Rights Amendment." *Smithsonian*. November 13, 2019. SmithsonianMag.com /history/equal-rights-amendment-96-years-old-and -still-not-part-constitution-heres-why-180973548.

US Equal Employment Opportunity Commission. "The Equal Pay Act of 1963." Accessed May 1, 2021. EEOC.gov/statutes /equal-pay-act-1963.

ABOUT THE AUTHOR

 **Carrie Floyd Cagle** lives in a suburb of Dallas, Texas, with her husband, daughter, and grumpy dachshund. When she's not writing history books, she loves to sew, bake, and binge-watch historical dramas. She has been a high school teacher for twenty years and has taught AP US History, AP Government, AP European History, AP Psychology, American history, and world history. Carrie has BAs in psychology and history and an MS in curriculum and instruction. Her social studies curriculum can be found online at bit.ly/ihearthistory.

CPSIA information can be obtained
at www.ICGtesting.com
Printed in the USA
JSHW050002170821
17898JS00003B/5